HOW TO MAKE MONEY FROM SOCIAL MEDIA MARKETING

STEPHEN AKINTAYO

HOW TO MAKE MONEY FROM SOCIAL MEDIA MARKETING

ABOUT THE AUTHOR

Stephen Akintayo is a Nigerian author and Digital Marketing Consultant, Entrepreneur, Business/Relationship Coach, TV/Radio Host and Philanthropist. He is currently the MD/CEO of Gtext Group, a leading firm in Nigeria whose services span from digital marketing, website design, bulk SMS, and online advertising, to media, e-commerce, real estate, consulting, and a host of other services.

He was born in Gonge Area of Maiduguri, Borno State, Nigeria to Mr. Victor and Mrs. Deborah Akintayo, in an impoverished environment with no electricity or potable drinking water. After his father's business crumbled, feeding became the biggest challenge of his family – whilst in primary school he scavenged for his lunch. His passion for philanthropy was birthed by his humble beginnings. In his words; "My surname was poverty. Hunger was my biggest challenge." Stephen spent the first twelve years of his life living in the forest of Maiduguri (along Danboa road). The living conditions were so bad that he slept on a mattress for the first time at the age of 13. As a result of the family's struggles, his primary school education was spotty.

Things got better in secondary school, though his mum had to borrow money each term to pay his school fees. His future looked very bleak. At 16, he read his first business book, *Rich Dad Poor Dad*, and that propelled him to his achievements. He started business a year later, selling GNLD food supplements (introduced to him by his cousin). Not long after, he ventured into his first online business, selling eBooks he bought for $10. From there, he did a dozen more businesses with varying degrees of success. His major inspiration for doing business was his mother. He wanted to succeed to compensate a very hard-working mother who denied herself everything in order to educate her 5 children. A day before hosting one of his most successful Student Trade Fairs, his mother died of ovarian cancer! This was the toughest season of his life and business career.

Stephen Akintayo's story is indeed a grass to grace one. His singular regret in life is that his hard-working mother died before she could witness some of the good works God is doing through him today. One of the companies he founded, Gilead Balm Group Services, has assisted a number of businesses in Nigeria to move to enviable levels by helping them reach their clients through its enormous nationwide database of real phone numbers and email addresses. It has hundreds of organizations as its clients including multinational companies like Guaranty Trust Bank, PZ Cussons, MTN, Chivita, amongst others.

He is also the Founder and President of Infinity Foundation and Stephen Akintayo Foundation, indigenous non-governmental organizations that assist orphans and vulnerable children as well as mentor young minds. The foundation has assisted over 2,000 orphans and vulnerable children and has also partnered with 22 orphanage homes in the country. In December 2015 he started Mercy Orphanage through Infinity Foundation to care for victims of Boko Haram insurgence in the Northern part of Nigeria. Stephen Akintayo Foundation focuses on Financial Grants with initial grant of $2,500 to 20 entrepreneurs in 2015, and plans to grow that to $1.4m annual grant by the 5th year; projects like Upgrade Conference and The Serial Entrepreneur Conference with thousands of attendees who benefit from high value knowledge from exceptional speakers and consultants.

Stephen is also the founder of Omonaija, an online radio station in Lagos currently streaming 24 hours daily. His first degree is in Microbiology from Olabisi Onabanjo University. He is a member of Institute of Strategic Management and a professional member of the Institute of Information Management – Africa. An ordained Pastor with Living Faith Church Worldwide, he is happily married to Mrs. Olabisi Akintayo and blessed with three children.

Copyright 2016

IMPORTANT LEGAL STUFF

Any perceived slight of specific people or organizations, and any resemblance to characters living, dead or otherwise, real or fictitious, is purely unintentional. You are encouraged to print this book for easy reading. However, you use this information at your own risk.

Contents

CHAPTER ONE

INTRODUCTION TO SOCIAL MEDIA MARKETING

INTRODUCTION TO SOCIAL MEDIA

"Marketing is no longer about the stuff you make, but about the stories you tell." –Seth Godin

Social media marketing has been known as one of the proven marketing strategies for some time now. This is why it is very important that as an entrepreneur, you utilize it maximally in order to increase your brand recognition.

Social media is a powerful tool for business, both on and offline. Whether you're new to internet marketing, or you're new and want to acquire knowledge on how to leverage social media to promote your business, then you are reading the right book.

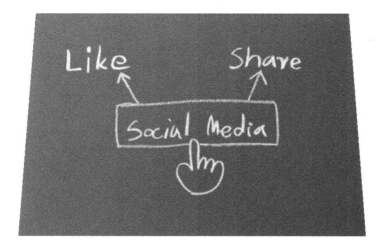

All over the world, over 3 billion people log on to various social media networks daily searching for one thing or the other which means that the internet is so vast that you can easily draw potential customers and give them the access to get in touch with you. In addition, the use of social media platforms allows you to become more recognizable both to your existing customers and their personal contacts, provided you are smart enough to get them to share or repost your content.

WHAT IS SOCIAL MEDIA MARKETING?

Social Media Marketing is the process of gaining website traffic or visitors through social media sites. Social media marketing campaigns usually center on efforts to create content that attracts attention and encourages readers to share them across their own social networks to their contacts.

The current trend of material postings is designed to enhance the exchange of idea where creativity has little or no bounds and the secure form of information is featured and accessed.

The sharing, collaboration and functionality of the social media allows for these to be done comfortably. This form of sharing is often done in an interactive fashion that also facilitates an immeasurable amount of viewpoints contributed.

Social media provides for the involvement and support one is able to garner through the exchange of ideas with likeminded individuals. Being open and honest as possible when participating is just as important as the material being designed to be posted.

However there is absolutely no need to conform in any way to the ideas and exchanges being feature as the social media platform exists for the honest exchange of ideas where other go to get information they need to address their own individual concerns and interests.

The various tools available such as blogging, social networking, podcasting and videos can be used to further the social media usage. Choosing one that most suits the needs on the individual will help to further the exploration of the social media tool and provide the necessary avenues for information exchange.

REASONS WHY SOCIAL MEDIA MARKETING IS IMPORTANT

Due to its high popularity ranking through the continual use, the social media tool has become a very important part of internet communication. This is also popularly considered a powerful venue for advertisers to create interest and traffic for their respective products or business endeavors.

Social media is a very important means of marketing that every online entrepreneur must endeavour to uutilize. The benefits of social media marketing include:

1. BRAND RECOGNITION

The internet is so large that you have to seize every opportunity you can to improve your brand recognition. Since social media networks are widely used these days all over the globe, using it to your advantage is a must. It can serve as a voice for your brand and can help you build your reputation and visibility.

Through social media, an entrepreneur can attract potential customers and it will be a lot easier for them to get in touch with them through this medium. Also, using social media platforms allows you to become more recognizable not only to your existing customers but to their personal contacts too, if they share or repost your content.

2. BETTER OPPORTUNITIES

Social media marketing also provides you with better opportunities in terms of converting potential customers to buying clients. Social media allows you to connect with an infinite web of relationships through your followers, existing contacts and target audience. By posting a video, a link to a blog, a campaign or perhaps a simple photo related to your business or any topic relevant to your company, you will be able to spark a reaction. Each of these reactions obtained from a single post is a chance for a possible conversion.

3. INCREASED TRAFFIC AND CONVERSION RATES

If you use social media marketing the right way, you can tremendously increase your website traffic and even your conversion rates. All this is made possible by social media because it promotes interaction between 2 individuals or a group. This interaction makes marketing more efficient. Inbound traffic to your site greatly increases as well since you will no longer be limited to potential customers belonging to your personal contacts and existing customers.

If you use the right social media marketing strategies, you'll be able to attract the existing members of your niche or followers in a specific social media platform that you've selected. This also gives you better chances of increasing your sales potential.

If you are not yet into social media marketing, you better start as soon as you can because the longer you wait, the more opportunities you are missing.

4. EXPAND YOUR REACH AND SPY ON YOUR COMPETITION

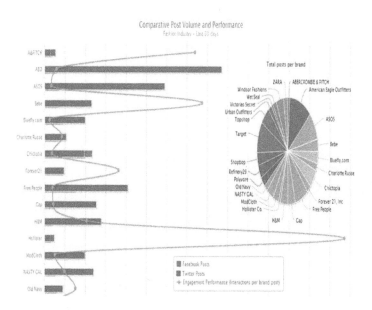

Apart from the benefit of engagement and building better relationships with your customers, you will also get to expand your reach without having to force your brand to your target audience. Commenting on live events creates content that is much more likely to be shared and hence go viral.

By following your competition, you can see what kind of deals they are offering customers, and keep up to date with other things they have going on. Just be sure that whatever you have to offer is better.

Examples of tools you can use to achieve this include SEO book, Marketing Trader, Topsy, Google alerts, SEMRush, SpyFu, etc.

5. BUILDING RELATIONSHIPS

Real time social media marketing will also pave the way for you to build relationships with your audience. This is probably one of the best things that you can get from this kind of strategy. You'll get to engage with your followers in real-time conversation which is very important if you wish to build on the trust of your customers and reputation of your brand.

Social media also allows you to build and enhance both personal and professional relationships. You can use it to connect with other industry experts, or find old friends from high school you're looking to reconnect with.

6. ESTABLISHING A BRAND AND RAISING AWARENESS

The Best Startup Practices to Raise

Through Social Media

The majority of people on the Internet today are using at least one social media network, such as Facebook, Twitter, or Instagram.

A good number of them are using two, or even all three of those social networks. Getting your brand out there on those platforms is a good way to let people know you are around.

MORE BENEFITS

Using the social media tool the individual is able to build a network of core supporters which is pivotal to the success of the site and its traffic garnering efforts.

This will provide the expansion needed to ensure the site is kept relevant and popular for the viewers. When the traffic generated is of a high volume then the other advantage to be reaped is in the rankings carried out by the SEOs.

With good rankings the individual is able to be better positioned for access by viewers and therefore be at the forefront of any search possibility because of the visibility and online exposure element.

With most people being concerned about the ecofriendly aspect of any endeavor, using the social media tool with adequately ensure this particular aspect is addressed.

As this form of reaching out to the customer does not require the use of actual tangible material such as paper and printing ingredients it is considered ecofriendly by comparison.

When the individual is able to attract a fairly strong following through the social media platform the follow up processes would then be much easier. Periodically reaching out to the loyal customer base with new information, products or services would be a welcomed element provided it is not abused in any way or overwhelming.

Establishing one's self as a formidable force on the social media circuit will create the following that will then ideally turn in to revenue for the individual.

The credibility built and the recognition gained will also facilitate the invitation to be featured on other sites as a guest and this will contribute further to avenues of spreading the individual's wares.

CHAPTER TWO

TYPES OF SOCIAL MEDIA PLATFORMS AND TOOLS USED FOR MARKETING

TYPES OF SOCIAL MEDIA PLATFORMS AND TOOLS USED FOR MARKETING

"We don't have a choice on whether we DO social media; the question is how well we DO it". –Erik Qualman

A social media platform is a web-based technology which enables the development, deployment and management of social media solutions and services. It provides the ability to create social media websites and services with complete social media network functionality.

TYPES OF SOCIAL MEDIA PLATFORMS

There are various social media platforms and tools experts use to promote their businesses online, advertise their goods and services and engage their customers. As an individual, business or organization wanting to make money or (more of) an impact through social media, on what platforms will you be active?

How will you allocate or divide your time between them? How can you make sense of the different demographics, purposes, and cultures of the major social media networks?

Some of these platforms include Twitter, Instagram, Facebook, Google+, LinkedIn, Blog, Tumblr, YouTube, and Pinterest. Examples of social media tools include Hootsuite, Buffer, Ninja blaster and many more.

1. TWITTER

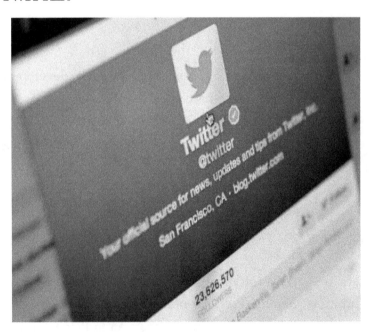

Providing mostly real time interaction, Twitter also has its contributing merits when it comes to using it as a tool for online business exposure.

Having the ability to reach the target audience in a nonthreatening environment, the parties involved will be able to conduct the interaction is a more comfortable and easy going manner which sometimes can be beneficial element for potential business introductions.

Twitter has its own unique branding and a nice way of social interaction. It's the ultimate social network when it comes to viral content. Twitter is home to the ever popular "hashtag" which has become a worldwide trend when it comes to posting catchy and interesting posts. The addition of celebrity users has also made it a handy form of entertainment. Twitter also has massive amounts of users which makes it a target for social media marketing.

BENEFITS OF USING TWITTER FOR SOCIAL MEDIA MARKETING

1. Research

With the use of hashtags making it easy to research nearly any topic imaginable, the built-in search feature is a valuable research tool. While the functionality will not replace the competitive research tools out there on the market today, it can help gather information about what's hot in the market, and where needs are within a particular niche.

2. Drive Traffic to Your Website

Many people will tweet about their new blog posts to their followers. However, just tweeting about your new blog post doesn't mean people will listen and click. For this to work, you need to be actively involved in the network, and share valuable information your network is interested in or is looking for.

3. Engage with Customers

The interaction element that Twitter effectively provides is an unmistakably important tool which can and should be explored for the definite merits.

Responding to tweets is a noninvasive way to presenting information that has been sought after in the first place.

Businesses can communicate with their customer base, and get feedback in a casual, and cost-effective way. Find out what your customers love (or hate) about what you have to offer, and make changes to improve it for them.

4. Networking

Twitter enables you to connect and communicate with friends and family, but it can also be a powerful professional networking tool. In addition, it can be a great way for employees within the same organization to communicate back and forth because it is so short and to the point.

5. Branding

Matching your Twitter handle to your business name, and using custom graphics on your Twitter profile can be a great way to reinforce your brand, and to help raise awareness in its early stages.

6. Maintaining a competitive edge

The Twitter platform is an excellent arena to keep track of what the individual's competitors are currently engaged in doing.

This will then allow the individual to use the information learnt to either improve on his or her contributions or come up with more innovative ways to garner a bigger share of the market.

HOW TO GET FOLLOWERS ON TWITTER

1. **Make sure what you post has value.** People will ignore you if it's garbage.

2. **Use hashtags.** This categorizes what you're talking about, which makes it easier for people to find.

3. **Tweet on one topic most of the time.** At least 80% of the time, talk about your business niche. This helps establish your credibility.

4. **Make use of your profile space.** Describe who you are, and provide a link to your website.

5. **Link to your profile from other social media profiles.** This helps people see that you are on Twitter.

6. **Include your Twitter link in your email signature.** This too, helps people know and see that you are on Twitter.

7. **Advertise your twitter link on your business cards.** This helps with offline marketing efforts and may bring additional followers.

8. **Use Twitter search.** Find people who you want to connect with. See who's talking about what, and jump in on the conversation.

9. **Use @s.** @twitterhandle lets you engage a person directly. Do this often!

10. **Use Follow Friday (#FF)** Not only will this help you suggest other people to your followers, you may find some awesome new connections this way.

11. **Follow friends of friends.** This can help you find other relevant followers to engage.

MAKING TWEETS

- **Share information of value.** Whether it's yours or not, share something you think your followers can use. You'll get more respect when you're not tooting your own horn all the time!
- **Use a URL shortener.** Something like bit.ly or owl.ly will shorten your URL to save you characters in your tweet, and it'll help you track the number of times it was clicked.
- **Use HootSuite or something similar.** Programs such as HootSuite and TweetDeck will allow you better manage your social media efforts. You can track several things on one screen, and even schedule tweets ahead of time, so you don't actually have to be in front of the screen to share information. Just be sure you're actively communicating with people who respond to your tweets.

ADVANTAGES OF TWITTER

- Using Twitter for marketing means you're able to contact your brand's biggest advocates directly, and they're able to contact you.

- Twitter is direct, compact, and simple to use. The character limit means you have to be concise. It's helpful for staying on the message and forces you to think clearly before posting something.

- Tweets are designed to spread quickly and easily, and there are multiple options. Tweets can be made a user's favorite, or can be retweeted, which posts your content directly in their timeline. It's very easy for content to go viral if you attract the right amount of attention, making Twitter marketing fast and effective.

- Hashtags offer simple indexing of content, making marketing on Twitter quick and concise. If you click on a hashtag, you'll see every tweet related to it, and the list will be updated in real time. A snapshot of how your campaign is working can be had with a simple click.

- Media such as photos and video are automatically embedded in the tweet, so fans can see the content without leaving the site.

DISADVANTAGES OF TWITTER

- The hard character limit can make it difficult to spread links and other information, especially if you're forced to be vague when you describe it. This can make it difficult to share sites with long URLs, and you'll need to factor that into your Twitter marketing strategy.

- Your Twitter feed can be hacked and used to spread misinformation or otherwise damage your brand. Twitter is seeking to fight this, using methods such as two-factor identification, but it's still a problem you'll need to account for using Twitter for business marketing. As a result of the hacking risks, users can be hesitant to click on links without a full address visible, even from brands they trust.

- Using Twitter for business can backfire. Hashtag campaigns can easily be hijacked by anybody from a competitor to activists, and once users decide to have fun at your expense, it can quickly get out of hand. A good example of this is McDonald's, which sponsored a hashtag only to see everyone from disgruntled employees to animal rights activists use it to embarrass the company. This can also draw negative media attention.

- If the wrong employee is put in charge of the Twitter feed, it can lead to a PR mess, whether it's a problem with an angry customer that gets out of hand or a very public expression of personal opinion. And as the Red Cross found out, there's the potential for very human mistakes. You'll need to weigh this risk in your Twitter marketing plan.

2. FACEBOOK

From its birth in 2004, Facebook has been a force to reckon with. By 2010, it became the most visited site on the entire web, ousting Google. Initially it was open to only college students, but it is now available for anyone's use. People can create profiles and connect with friends. Businesses can also make use of it to create pages to connect with their customers and advertise their products and services online. Facebook keeps getting richer, as a user experience and as a place for businesses to build communities and advertise for customers. The site continues to grow because new users, merely curious at first, often become addicted to it.

Almost everyone you relate with is on Facebook which means that they are your potential buyers. Facebook itself has embraced the fact that their social media platform can and will be used as a critical resource for social media marketing. The opportunities are limitless.

BENEFITS OF USING FACEBOOK FOR SOCIAL MEDIA MARKETING

1. CONNECTING AND BUILDING RELATIONSHIPS

Facebook offers both a live chat and a private message platform that can be used to connect with clients, colleagues, and prospects. Savvy Internet markets will use this feature to create and nurture relationships.

2. BUILDING BRAND CREDIBILITY

Your business page will allow you to share as much information as you want. Logos and pictures can be used to fortify brand awareness. You also can use the page to share your core brand message with fans, and by interacting with fans, you're sharing your message with all their friends and followers as well.

How to Set Up Your Fan Page on Facebook

While you likely already have a Facebook account for personal use, using a real profile for business and promotion is against the Facebook terms and conditions, so it is important that you create a fan page for your product/service.

1. Visit Facebook.com/page

2. Select your category from the list of options:

a. Local Business or Place

b. Company, Organization or Institution

c. Brand or Product

d. Artist, Band or Public Figure

e. Entertainment

f. Cause or Community

3. **Fill in Information:** Business name, location, website, date launched/founded, hours of operation, etc.

4. **Add Photos**

5. **Suggest the Page to Your Friends:** This is a good way to get a jump on the number of likes you have, to start spreading your message and brand presence.

6. **Import Contacts:** Import email contacts to suggest your page to people you know who are not your Facebook friends.

7. **Start Writing Content:** Post status updates, share links, etc., to start engaging your fan base. When you have enough fans, get a vanity URL so it becomes easier to remember/advertise.

How to get likes on Facebook

- **Regularly post a status update.** Tag your business page in it and ask your friends to like the page, and share it with their friends.
- **Get fans to upload and tag photos.** Encourage your fans to upload and tag photos of themselves with your business page.
- **Offer an incentive.** Whether it's a discount on your products or services, or a free eBook/report related to your industry, people will be more likely to like your page when they get something in return.

- **Install a page badge.** This is a quick, easy way to link your Facebook page.
- **Install a Facebook "Like Box" on your website.** This enables website visitors become your Facebook fans without having to visit Facebook itself, or leave your website.
- **Install a "Like" button on your website.** When users click this, your website (or blog posts, or whatever they click) will show up in their stream, advertising you to their friends.
- **Connect the page to Twitter.** Anything you post to Facebook will be posted to Twitter, allowing you to convert your Twitter followers into Facebook fans.
- **List your page as a place of employment.** This enables you to link to your page on your personal profile.
- **Include your Facebook page URL in your email signature and on your business cards.** This is a good way to promote offline.
- **Provide a link to your Facebook page when you leave blog comments.** This will build back links to help you increase your rank. Plus, when people see the comment, they can click and may like your page.
- **Provide a link to your Facebook page on your profile.** It keeps the link visible to your friends who do not "like" your page already.
- **Run a "fans only" contest.** People will become fans just to get in on the contest prize.

- **Advertise your page.** Use Facebook advertising to promote your page to people outside your network. You may run across companies out there promoting fans for purchase. This is typically a practice we shy away from recommending, because the fans are generally fake profiles, and even if they are real people, they are not likely to be targeted customers. You're much better off with a smaller fan base that's more likely to listen to you or make a purchase from you, than a higher fan base that doesn't convert to sales for you. Use this tactic at your own risk.

FACEBOOK ADVERTISING

The greatest thing about advertising with Facebook, is the flexibility of your advertisements.

You can customize your advertisements so they appear only to specific groups or segments of people based on the information contained within their profile or based on gender, location or personal preferences.

For example, if your product is tailored towards single mothers, you could develop your advertisements so that they are triggered to appear only for those who have indicated that they are single mothers in their profiles, or who have demonstrated interest in similar products or services based on their personal profile, communities or groups they've joined, or other advertisements they've responded to.

- **Create Targeted Advertisements**

In order to create the most compelling, responsive and profitable advertisements, you need to utilize Facebook's option to heavily target and tailor your advertisements based on your target market.

With Facebook, you can set your ads up so that they appear only to specific people, based on age, location, gender, interests, hobbies or even based on the groups they have joined within the Facebook community.

You will want to conduct market research so that you can accurately define your target market and develop advertisements that target specific segments of your market.

Facebook implores a quality control system to ensure that the advertisements that run throughout their community stay within their guidelines and do not offend or disrupt member activity or overall experience.

Use their quality control system to develop compelling advertisements that stand out in the marketplace, and capture the attention of potential buyers.

Also keep in mind that Facebook advertising is based on display, rather than search. This means that your ads will be automatically triggered to appear based on your settings, rather than when a user conducts an on-site search.

Users can also choose to rate advertisements, helping to retain quality throughout the community.

- **<u>Improve your Click Through Rate</u>**

Your advertisements click through rate plays an integral role in saving you money while boosting exposure and reaching out to your target market. It's important to keep a pulse on your click through rate so that you can correct any problems with your advertisement, or make adjustments to improve your overall CTR.

If your advertisements CTR drops too low, it could be automatically paused or removed by Facebook, so you really want to pay attention to how well it's converting.

Typically, your ads should never fall below a 2% conversion rate.

One of the easiest ways of increasing your CTR is by creating a highly targeted advertisement.

You want your ad to appear only to those who are within your target demographic, while making sure that your advertisements text or any images used speak directly to your customer base.

Consider split testing various advertisements within the Facebook community to determine what works best, based on your industry or niche market.

You should also pay attention to the times of day that your ads appear. You can choose to either run your ads consistently throughout the day, or have them only appear at specific times (or even specific dates).

Keep in mind the time zone of your target market, so that your ads are running based on the most active time of day or night.

- **Stay Within Facebook Guidelines.**

It's important to understand how Facebook advertising channels work, and what is permitted as well as what is not allowed within the marketplace.

Facebook is very flexible with the types of advertisements that are allowed to be displayed within their community, however they do not allow images or text that may be considered offensive.

- **Setting Your Maximum Daily Bid**

One of the most important aspects of setting up an effective Facebook advertisement is in the maximum daily bid that you are willing to pay. The higher your daily bid, the more exposure your ad will receive.

You want to start off with a lower bid if you are just getting used to advertising with Facebook, and increase your maximum daily bid as you fine-tune your advertisements for maximum results.

It's important to always keep a pulse on how well your advertisement is converting, so that you can improve click through rates and overall response.

When you create an advertisement with Facebook, they will suggest a maximum bid based on your advertisements focus and target market (based on your personal configuration and preferences).

You can start off by setting your maximum daily bid slightly lower than what's suggested and increase it as you improve your advertisements conversion rates so that you are getting the most bang for your buck!

- **CPC versus Impression Based Ads**

With Facebook, you can develop advertisements where you either pay for impressions or based on the number of clicks your ad receives.

If you are just getting started with Facebook advertising, I recommend choosing cost per click (CPC), so that you can accurately test your advertisements, while paying only for responses rather than just views.

You can always change your advertisement format to 'impression based' later on in the event you wish to test out alternative options.

Much like a Google Ad campaign, Facebook has a platform that allows you to pay for ads based on impressions (the number of times they are served) or clicks (the number of times the ad is clicked on.) Using Facebook's ad platform, you can target your ads based on any number of demographics, including: age, location, gender, marital status, interests, etc.

You can set a budget, and when you reach that budget, stop running the ad. The ads are served either on the sidebar of the page, or could be used as a sponsored story. You will have to bid on cost per click, so the lower your bid, the less likely your ad is to be served. The first time you run an ad, it will be approved by Facebook before going live.

Announcing important events.

Using your Facebook page, you can announce events, such as conferences, appearances, schedules, product launches, discounts, and other special promotion. Fans can recommend the event to friends, to help spread your message further.

3. GOOGLE +

The Google+ play is not about bringing ads to the social network- it's about bringing social media to the world's biggest ads platform. Google+ is ideal for content sharing. It is compatible with YouTube. The Google+ hangouts function, circles and communities all make brand awareness and content marketing simple.

Google+ is an individual friendly platform. The communities function works well to give businesses from all sectors a place to find like-minded individuals and businesses. If you are interested in learning more about your field, then Google+ is a place you can do that.

The Benefits of an Active Presence on Google+

The features unique to Google+ are what make it valuable to businesses. These features help an organization stand out from their competitors, reap the benefits of the platform and perform better across their website, social and search.

These features include:

- **Google+ Hangouts:** Many businesses have created either their own series of Google+ Hangouts or have held multiple, one-time events as a Hangout. Hangouts enable businesses to discuss topics of interest to their audience face to face, while including the input of others to ensure that an engaging conversation is occurring. A Hangout can drive long-term loyalty with your Google+ community because your business is able to showcase its human side and interact with audience members in real-time. Take a look at Bake Space or National Geographic Travel for examples of businesses with well-executed Google+ Hangouts.

- **Search Engine Optimization:** Google+ acts as a social layer to all other Google properties, connecting an individual's actions across all these products into one profile. Because of this, the activity of your company's page on Google+ can directly affect your website's rankings in Google search. Sharing content, building your following, interacting with others, hosting Hangouts and the other activity occurring on your Google+ page can affect how your content ranks in search. Your Google+ content will show up more frequently for people logged into their Google account with your page in their circles.

- **Gmail Integration:** Google+ is linked to all Google products, and Gmail is no exception. When your business sends emails to your list, the latest post from your Google+ page will appear on the top right-hand side of the dashboard of all recipients using Gmail. This integration is another way for your business to spur more interactions with your existing audience by using content already shared on Google+.

- **Circles:** The way an audience on a Google+ page is segmented is by choosing which users your business wishes to place in each circle based on your own groupings. For example, segment audience members you're posting to by loyal customers, press, new customers, fans of product line #1, fans of product line #2, etc. Circles offer businesses the ability to segment their audiences similar to the way they would their email lists, delivering the most relevant information to each portion of their audience based on their preferences.

- **Communities:** Similar to the ideas of groups on other social networks, Google+ communities allow users to come together to discuss and share content based on specific topics of interests. Only certain topics can be discussed in these communities since the owners can heavily moderate them. Community owners and moderators can be individuals, a business page or both. These communities enable a business to facilitate conversations and the creation of user-generated content on a subject related to their offerings.

- **YouTube Integration:** Google+ is tightly synched with your YouTube channel, showcasing your video content on both properties for one consistent experience. When hosting a Hangout on Air, the event video will be reposted to your YouTube channel for future benefit to your audience. It's critical to have these two social platforms connected to reap the full benefits of their use in consolidating and optimizing your video content.

- **Google Authorship:** The writers who create content for your business need to set up authorship on their individual Google+ profiles to help drive greater visibility to your content. Author Rank is an algorithm that Google will eventually take into consideration regarding an author's published content and how it appears in the search results. Google+ allows authors to verify ownership of their content to claim it as their own and begin to associate themselves as a credible source on various subjects. By requiring that your content creators set up Google Authorship on Google+, you'll be more likely to gain long-term content visibility in search engines.

- Lastly, the Google+ audience tends to be comprised of more tech savvy users, as compared to Facebook. This is beneficial to your business because your audience is more likely to participate in Google Hangouts and respond to the use of the social network's unique feature sets. The more a business knows about their audience on a network, the more able they'll be to create content and conversations that resonate with that user base with features specific to Google+.

The Downsides of an Active Presence on Google+

- **Similarities to Facebook:** One of the major downsides of being active on Google+ is that it is very similar to Facebook in the way a user interacts with the platform to share content. A recent Forrester report highlighted how a few brands simply replicate content from their Facebook on to Google+ and it performs well.

This isn't the ideal approach to either social network. Each community should be treated as unique with content tailored to increase their interactions with your organization. Nevertheless, some well-known brands have found that the platforms are similar enough that they can get away with this tactic.

To avoid this, alter an aspect of a post you're sharing on Google+ by formatting the copy with some of the rich formatting options like bolding, italicizing or strikethroughs. See this Google+ cheat sheet to understand how to best accomplish this unique formatting.

Additionally, add more text to your updates. Google+ users react better to longer posts in their feed as opposed to Facebook users in the newsfeed. Aim to create a content strategy that differentiates your content on the network from content elsewhere.

- **Limitations of SEO:** Content from Google+ shows up less frequently when a person doesn't have your page in his or her circles or is not logged in. This limits the effectiveness of the SEO benefits of a Google+ page that is often touted as a major impact of the social network.

This means that anyone not logged into their Google account will be less likely to see a Google+ page's content in the search results. This relates to the personalization that users experience in their Google search results. Results vary depending on users and their actions across their Google profiles.

To get around this limitation, it's important to build a relevant Google+ audience even if they aren't particularly active on the network because they will more likely see your content in search results.

- **No Contests or Promotions:** Unlike other social media networks, the Google+ contests and promotions policy prohibits businesses from hosting contests or promotions on Google+ pages. This policy is obviously limiting since one of the many beneficial ways to increase engagement is by hosting contests, giveaways and promotions.

To maneuver around this policy, your company can post links to a contest or promotion occurring on one of your other channels. These promotions simply can't be hosted on Google+ or involve any Google features as a means of entry.

- **Lack of Market Share:** There is undoubtedly potential with Google+, a large network of 540 million monthly active Google+ users and many success stories, yet many people still don't use the service. Let's be honest, how many people do you know who actively use Facebook,

Twitter and other social networks but don't use their Google+ at all?

Google+ may be able to inflate their user numbers to make the social network appear more active, but could a significant amount of this activity on the channel be pulled from interactions on Gmail, YouTube and Google's other products?

Many questions remain to be answered and lots of potential to be fulfilled on the network, but one of the major disadvantages of the platform is that many people are just not actively using the channel after they were forced to set it up as a part of the use of other Google products.

What businesses should be on Google+?

Tech and engineering companies as well as marketing individuals. The top three brands on Google+ are Android, Mashable and Chrome, with Android leading the pack by a significant margin. Below are few facts to know about Google+:

- Google+ users are 67% male
- The majority are in technical and engineering fields.
- The average age, somewhat surprisingly, is 28.

Although the platform boasts 540 million users, only 300 million or so are active (the huge number of users can be put down, in large, part, to Google's purchase of YouTube in 2006).

4. PINTEREST

Pinterest is derived from two separate words, pin and interest. It is a web and mobile application company that operates a photo sharing website. It has defined itself as "the world's catalog of ideas" or a visual discovery, collection and storage tool.

Pinterest was founded by Ben Silbermann, together with Paul Sciarra and Evan Sharp, in March 2010 and is now a huge success, making it one of the top social media networks. It is considered as the darling of social media.

Nine months after the launch, Pinterest already had 10,000 users registered. It slowly started to get noticed by magazines and started to make appearances in articles. In December 2011, the site became one of the top largest social network services.

Pinterest's demographics are interesting, and not just because it's so astoundingly female-dominated. It has the second-highest percentage of internet users in the 50,000+/year income bracket, and 34% of Pinterest users have a household income of 100,00+. Below are few facts about Pinterest:

- Pinterest has, in the past year, vaulted its way to the number 3 spot as most popular social media platform
- 21% of all US adults use it.
- 84% of those users are female - which makes it the second most popular site by far for this demographic.
- Pinterest is 80% more viral and 3x more effective at generating leads than Twitter
- The popularity of Pinterest spans multiple generations

In fact, Pinterest has far and away the best ROI for those businesses that fit its demographic base. 70% of Pinterest users use the platform to get inspiration on what to buy (compared to, for instance, 17% on Facebook). So, if your business fits - your business should most definitely sit.

A report from Piqora in November found that the average Pin has a real-world value of 78 cents - making it by far the most valuable social media action that users can take.

The same report found that each pin drove, on average, two website visits and six page-views. This is especially interesting given that last year, jewelry retailer, Boticca, found that Pinterest traffic to their website spent, on average, more than twice as much as traffic from Facebook ($180 vs. $85). And Sephora went further, saying Pinterest users spent 15x as much as Facebook users.

Pinterest is perfect for ecommerce businesses, as not only is a pin worth more than any other social endorsement, they stay influential for a substantially longer period of time. This is because, with Pinterest, users simply keep scrolling down their search results (as the page is never ending)

Here are some of the common misconceptions about Pinterest:

- Only women are on Pinterest (females still make up the majority of the audience though)

- People only pin food and wedding content (travel, clothing, home decor are big too)

- My target audience isn't on Pinterest

- I don't have time for another social network

Top six reasons to utilize Pinterest for your business.

1. *Pinterest converts more browsers into buyers.*

Pinterest helps to reduce the number of steps from discovery to conversion, making it easier for people to get straight to the source. Visitors from Pinterest are more likely to convert into leads or sales faster than from other social media sources. Way to go, Pinterest!

Sometimes it's good to think of Pinterest as a big, visual search engine. People often turn to it during the research phase of their planning. They also turn to Pinterest for inspiration. I'm pretty sure most of us have tried at least one recipe for Pinterest.

2. *Pinterest drives traffic (and lots of it).*

Pinterest is an excellent tool to help increase links back to your website, which, in turn, drives more traffic. It is more effective at steering traffic back to a website more than any other social media source. (Thank you, rich pins!)

This uptick in traffic obviously relies on good content. If you're creating and sharing content that your audience likes, they're more likely to follow your links. Good content on Pinterest starts with creating quality visuals.

3. *Pins get you more inbound links.*

Because every pin includes a link, it makes it easy to lead it back to the source of the image. Just think of how many visitors you can bring to your website by posting images of your products on Pinterest. This is an often forgotten part of Pinterest. Never underestimate the power of image search!

4. *User engagement is ridiculously high.*

Users on Pinterest seem pretty content to simply find and share things with small groups of people. This is good for your business! Why? It means that your pins are more likely to be seen, touched, and even go viral!

5. *Pinterest integrates with your website, Facebook profile, and Twitter account.*

Why is this a good thing? Because it enables users to automatically post new pins to their news feeds for others to see. Although we're not big fans of cross-platform posting, many people find it helpful. If you're relying on automation, you might be trying to do too much. You might want to spend some time on a social media strategy first.

6. *Discover what your audience loves.*

One of the beautiful things you can do with Pinterest is use it to see what is trending *right now.* Follow anyone who follows you to see what inspires them – you will have a first-person look into their mind. Pinterest gives you the opportunity to see and understand what's hot today and use that information to position your offers and products.

Disadvantages of using Pinterest

- The main advantage of Pinterest can also be its biggest disadvantage: it relies on images. That means you need to be very mindful of the images you post because it is the images that will attract followers. Poor pictures will have people that follow you skip past you in their feed and not read the message in your description.

- There is no protection functionality to prevent others from stealing your images stored in a user account. Along those same lines, Pinterest makes it too easy to steal other people's work.

- There is a lesser range of men who are Pinterest users. 81% are female which means your business designed for men may not totally succeed.

- The search function often turns up completely unrelated items to what is being searched. This may be more related to the fact of mis-tagging the pins.

- If your image does not sell, you pin will not be clicked on. Pinterest relies entirely on looks and not really text to sell ideas. You could have a great product but it can be easy to misrepresent what you offer in Pinterest.

Which businesses should be on Pinterest?

Fashion, photographers, jewelers, home-hardware stores (DIY). The female-dominated, image-dominated facts of Pinterest make it easy for those brands which naturally lend themselves in that direction, and very difficult for those brands which don't.

5. INSTAGRAM

The most important factor for Instagram marketers are the age demographics. Although only 17% of US adults are on the site, a full 43% of mobile owners aged 18-29 are on the site.

Coming up fast behind Twitter is Instagram, with 17% of US adults on the site.

Interestingly, with Instagram, though it's the fifth most-popular social media platform, it has the second most devoted users.

- Instagram is the only platform that is actually skewed towards blacks and Hispanics.
- 57% of users access the site on a daily basis, only 6 points behind Facebook, and 11% ahead of third-place Twitter.

Which businesses should be on Instagram?

Image-friendly businesses like restaurants, clothes and fashion, food, architecture, technology, designers, etc. Because of the dominance of the 18-29 age group on Instagram, businesses with that target market should also be on the site.

Remember that Instagram users are all amateur-photographers, so you can't just snap an image of your newest dessert and expect it to go viral. Put time and energy into your images and you'll get far better engagement than otherwise.

If you're struggling for content for your Instagram profile, just think about making your business look awesome. Show the fun stuff you're doing, how exciting and innovative your office is. Also pay close attention to current events and holidays, as Instagram (like Twitter) is closely involved in what's trending.

Key Benefits of Using Instagram

There are lots of perks that Instagram can generate for your business, so let's have a look at the top 6 key benefits.

1. Increased Engagement

Depending on the quality of the post, branded updates on Facebook and Twitter are sometimes overlooked by the user. However this isn't true for Instagram users; having an active Instagram account with useful and interesting content can earn you crazy levels of engagement with your audience. A current study revealed that Instagram content generates 58 times more engagement per follower than Facebook and 120 times more than Twitter.

2. Building Trust and Personality

With branded content being more popular for generating engagement, one of the key benefits of Instagram is that it can help you build trust. People buy from people and Instagram will help you to create that emotional connection with your audience. The great thing here is that it allows you to share the day-to-day experiences of your business in an informal and casual way – therefore giving a personal feel to your business.

Behind the scene photos and employee images tend to rank well on Instagram, especially if you're a specific service provider. Such photos can make your company more attractive and trustworthy which in turn can have a positive effect on your bottom line.

3. Increase in Traffic

Although you can't add clickable links to every Instagram update you publish, Instagram can be a powerful source of traffic. Plus with the higher levels of engagement than on Facebook and Twitter, creating and maintaining a strong profile could be hugely beneficial for your site's visibility.

4. Gaining a Competitive Advantage

There is still far less competition on Instagram than on Facebook or Twitter. An American Express survey showed that only 2% of small businesses are currently embracing Instagram, giving them an advantage over their competitors. Plus the businesses that incorporate Instagram into their marketing strategy will more likely reach their target audience far easier than with Facebook or Twitter where the competition is much bigger.

5. Reaching Target Market

If you're targeting people born from 1980 to the early 1990s (the so called millennial) then Instagram is the place to be as over 37% of people in this age group use Instagram. So if you want to reach and connect with the under 30 crowd you should definitely create an Instagram account. Having said that, Instagram doesn't only work for youth-focused brands like Red

Bull; brands like Ford and General Electric are gaining a great level on engagement on their Instagram profiles.

6. Free Advertising

Yes, you're reading it correctly; the great thing about Instagram is free advertising. You can showcase your products and services in action which generates huge exposure. It gives you a chance to show off more of what you have to offer.

What Are the Cons of Instagram for Business?

1. Your targeted demographics might not even have an Instagram account.

Instagram is a social platform that is dominated by the younger age demographics. Although older users are exploring Instagram with more frequency, it's a good bet that the average viewer is going to be young, with limited discretionary spending, and that may not be who you want hearing your brand message right now.

2. It is not always a platform that focuses on commerce.

There are plenty of reasons to follow someone on Instagram. It might be a fun way to connect to a favorite celebrity. Or it might be a way to share images of your kids and stay connected with family. The idea of shopping for items by following accounts on Instagram isn't quite there yet as a priority for everyone. Many people log into Instagram to pass the time and have no intentions of buying anything.

3. Advertising may be out of reach for most businesses.

Most businesses are forced to rely on organic traffic when it comes to Instagram for business. Only the largest brands can typically afford to advertise on this platform, which means it can take some time to develop a following that has a meaningful impact on your budget. Although video ads cost just $0.02 per view, that can translate to up to $1 million per month for some campaigns.

4. There isn't much room for additional content.

Some images require a little explanation, but Instagram doesn't offer much space to make that happen. It's also difficult to create a comprehensive company bio on this platform, which makes it a little hard for followers to get to know who you really are. This means the brand message you put forth is generally through images or videos only, and that can be a fairly expensive proposition if you're wanting professional-quality uploads.

5. It can be easy for a brand message to go off course.

Because this is such a visual medium, it can be tempting for businesses to try different techniques to attract new followers and business opportunities that fall outside of their established brand message. You must stay true to the personality of your brand so that your Instagram account is authentic. If you allow your message to go off course, then you can push a significant number of potential customers out of the picture, so to speak.

6. Most users access Instagram from a mobile device.

Although the saturation of mobile device ownership is ever increasing, not every potential customer currently owns one. This can make it difficult to reach customers who might be far enough along in your sales funnel that they're willing to make a purchase. Some businesses may discover that many of their online consumers will be left out if the marketing focus is Instagram only.

The pros and cons of Instagram for business show that the positives will generally outweigh the negatives, but some steps must be taken to ensure success. You must focus on your experiences, showcasing the visual beauty your products or services have to offer. There must be an effort to get to know your followers. Each post must incite some sort of action. If you can do that, then you can meet your goals thanks to what Instagram is able to provide.

6. LINKEDIN

Only 13% of LinkedIn users are signing in daily. People use the platform to check up on business partners, find jobs, and occasionally network - things they do periodically, rather than on an hourly basis like hardcore users of Twitter, Instagram and Facebook.

It is this, despite holding the number 2 spot as world's most popular social media platform, that makes LinkedIn notoriously difficult to find success with for businesses. Below are a few facts about LinkedIn:

- The platform touts itself as the 'professional social network', and in that respect it's accurate.
- 38% of internet users with an income of more than $75k are on the platform.
- 79% of LinkedIn users are aged 35 or older, making it the oldest platform in this list.
- 27% of employed Americans are using the platform as well.

The three dominant sectors on the platform are high tech (14.3%), finance (12.4%) and manufacturing (10.1%). Worth noting is that the legal sector makes up a meager 1.4% of users.

The site also offers custom options, like display advertising, sponsorships of specific, LinkedIn groups, and dedicated e-mail marketing campaigns. About the dedicated email campaigns, Tom Funk says, "Before my 20th college reunion, my alma mater, Middlebury College, sent a highly personalized e-mail pitch to remind me to register to attend the reunion. The email pictured all the people in my professional network on LinkedIn who also happened to have been classmates of mine in the

Middlebury class of 1987. The execution of this email, and the technology that drove it, were pretty impressive and high impact. What better engagement technique for getting a person to read and react to an e-mail than to display profile head shots of the reader's friends? Sure enough, I opened it, scanned the faces with interest, read the e-mail, and felt nostalgic enough to register for the event then and there".

LinkedIn is increasingly losing the business networking battle to Google+, whose Community tool is, somewhat inexplicably, winning next to LinkedIn's groups (despite them being very similar in nature).

LinkedIn doesn't have the same 'fun' factor that many of the other platforms have. It's not about spending an hour scrolling through your ex-girlfriend's pictures from South East Asia, or about adding a filter to your New Year's pictures, or chiming in on the latest development between Kim Kardashian and... (I don't even know, Justin Bieber?).

LinkedIn is for professionals, and it's about professionals. It's hugely influential in the job hunt, both for employers and applicants. It's great for networking, and the content sharing function is getting better on a weekly basis. However, is it a revenue-generating platform like Pinterest and Instagram or a brand awareness increase-er like Facebook and Twitter? I'd say no. But feel free to convince me!

What Are the Pros of LinkedIn for Business?

1. It improves the SEO profile of a small business.

Search engines today look for value. Sometimes this is found in content. At other times it is found by how often content is shared with others. With LinkedIn for Business, professionals get the chance to hit both of these key points. They can create content which is directly shared on the social platform, which can then be shared as an article link on other social sites like Facebook or Twitter. This means the most crucial bits of information have increased internet exposure and this can lead to better overall conversion rates.

2. It is an easy way to stay up-to-date within an industry.

Whether a small business owner wants the latest information on their products or services or someone just has a passing interest in a certain subject, LinkedIn for Business helps to keep everyone in the loop. You have instant access to every upcoming trend or idea that is being talked about right now. As an added benefit, you can also become part of the conversation where people within the same industry share their own experiences or lend advice.

3. It is a cost-effective networking venture.

For people who are on a limited budget, LinkedIn for Business offers a basic account for free that can help to build a professional identity. It allows people to build a network that they trust as well. Free accounts are even allowed to request up to 5 introductions at one time and get weekly alerts on saved searches. Even if you want a premium account, the cost can be less than $600 per year.

4. You know specific information about customer and/or industry segments.

When you have specific data about what people want, then you know how to create something of value. This is the cornerstone of any potential business opportunity. This also provides a secondary advantage as it gives people the information needed to find new business partners, recruit new employees, and ultimately reduce overhead costs.

5. It provides a chance to offer niche expertise.

People today gravitate toward whomever has the most influential data to share. The internet is filled with information and much of it isn't accurate. Maybe you've heard the statistic that 90% of the statistics you'll find online are made up? Thanks to the answers program within LinkedIn for Business, you get the chance to show off the niche expertise you have within your industry without the need to develop your own site. In return, you get an affordable boost to your credibility.

6. Company information can be researched for literally nothing.

Whether your focus is B2B or B2C, companies have a chance to research anyone without spending anything. This can let you know if a potential business opportunity that seems a little too good to be true really is, or if it could be a dream investment. Add in the global access that LinkedIn for Business provides and even foreign direct investments and other methods of portfolio expansion which require due diligence to be performed are easier to complete.

7. It is a fast way to establish personal credibility.

LinkedIn for Business allows customers and partners to offer testimonials regarding your activities. Virtually any data can be shared that can make individuals and businesses look good. Company contacts can also be included with this information so that when someone encounters a positive testimonial or locates skills that are needed for an upcoming project, they can reach out immediately to begin the relationship-building process.

8. It enhances your visibility.

In many ways, any professional who wants to get noticed online needs to have a LinkedIn for Business account. There's no better way to enhance personal visibility in the white noise of data the internet provides. Even if all you're trying to do is find a job, you'll become easier to find when you have an active and optimized account. You still have privacy with this advantage as well because you can mask your network so your data can't be mined by others.

What Are the Cons of LinkedIn for Business?

1. You are going to receive tons of spam messaging.

Not every message you receive when on this social platform is going to be useful. When you start using LinkedIn for Business to advance your own cause, you'll find others are going to do the same with you. Not only must you filter out all of this spam, which takes time, but you've also got to make sure that your own valuable expertise isn't being deleted by others because it's being seen as spam as well.

2. It requires a large initial time investment.

Not every business professional is active on LinkedIn. It can take time for connections to form and conversations to get started. You'll spend much of your initial time with introductions as you work on building connections. This process can be tedious and sometimes even unsuccessful. Premium accounts can help limit the time investment, but that also means making a monetary investment that some small business owners or individuals might not be ready to make.

3. Many people use LinkedIn for Business to sell.

Sometimes networking is about making a sale, but more often than not it is about forming a relationship. You'll find that many of the initial connections you might be making are wanting you to buy something instead. Even when networking, you still have to do some selling because your connections typically must introduce you to people you may know. Premium accounts can avoid some of this, but not all of it.

4. Networking interactivity is rather limited compared to other social platforms.

If you're used to Facebook or Twitter and you come over to LinkedIn for Business, then you're going to be in for quite a surprise. Interactions are rather limited on the site. You're going to spend more time working up your profile than you are making comments, creating posts, and the other methods of interaction you're used to having on other sites.

5. LinkedIn for Business doesn't always happen in real time.

You have no predictability as to when someone will be online with their LinkedIn for Business account. Hundreds of millions of people log into Facebook every day and over 1.3 billion people use it once per month. When you're making a business connection through LinkedIn, however, you might find some connections take 6 months or more to get back with you.

6. There's no guarantee that someone has the expertise they claim.
LinkedIn for Business allows others to endorse people and the skills which they have, but someone who is new to the site isn't going to have any endorsements at all. This means there may be no guarantees that the network you are forming is actually going to be a beneficial network. You'll also find this rule applies

to you – until you start receiving independent endorsements of your skills, many professionals are going to operate with caution around you.

7. Breaking up the premium accounts into monthly charges is even more expensive.

A business premium account might cost less than $600, but that's only if you pay the annual charge in one lump sum. If you need to break down the charges into a monthly payment, you could find yourself paying $59.99 per month + any taxes required for the account. That's an extra $119.98 that could be funneled into other opportunities.

8. LinkedIn for Business searches can pull in negative personal data.

Did you leave a negative review on Yelp? Or make a comment of Facebook that in retrospect maybe shouldn't have been left? LinkedIn for Business has a high domain authority, which means related content to the individual or business with an account is going to display in searches. The chances of something negative being seen are generally quite small, but it is still a possibility. You may wish to delete items which could be seen as questionable.

The pros and cons of LinkedIn for Business show that it can be a very beneficial development and outreach process. It can also help to improve conversion rates, find good employees, and naturally increase sales over the long-term. If you're looking to network outside of a business purpose, however, you may find that other platforms, such as Facebook and Twitter, are going to provide better networking opportunities.

Which businesses should be on LinkedIn?

All professionals should be on LinkedIn, as individuals. I also recommend all professional businesses to be on LinkedIn, though the effort you need to maintain your presence there is significantly less than other platforms. Check in periodically to ensure your profile is stable - but focus your valuable time and energy on the more revenue-generating or awareness-increasing platforms.

There is room for some small businesses to start a conversation or become a trusted source of information with the groups function. I'd recommend all freelance marketers, bloggers, journalists, designers, etc., to have a significant presence on LinkedIn.

LinkedIn supports business pages, modeled somewhat on Facebook pages but less robust. These are no-cost, and they are worth setting up to familiarize yourself more with the platform, to stake out your territory, and to create a destination page should you want to kick the tires on advertising.

CHAPTER THREE

HOW TO CREATE SOCIAL MEDIA CAMPAIGNS THAT WORK

HOW TO CREATE SOCIAL MEDIA CAMPAIGNS THAT WORK

"A brand is no longer what we tell the customer it is – it is what customers tell each other it is". –Scott Cook

P eople all over the globe connect through social media and indeed we can call this a magnificent technological revolution. Connecting with other people on a personal note and for business purposes is now easier than it ever was. The internet has now turned into a vast marketplace and social media plays an important part in it. If you wish to have a successful social media campaign that is not only solid in theory but actually works, then you definitely have to check out the 5 tips discussed below:

1. Select the right platform

Choosing the correct platform for your niche is far more important than opting for the best one in the market right now.

This means that if Facebook is in, it does not automatically mean that it is the right one for your business. You can choose from a wide selection of social media sites namely Twitter, Pinterest, Facebook, YouTube and smaller niche social networks. There are several other new sites that are emerging as of the moment. Take the time to find the right platform for your company and consider even the newer and smaller ones. Once you have figured this out, choose a small target audience for your campaign and start from there.

2. Analytical tools are vital

You should always monitor how your campaigns are doing. With the help of analytical tools, you'll get to keep track of your posts, images or videos and see how they are performing. You can even check which ones are being shared to others the most. Several third-party programs will help you do this and using some of the best ones will help you monitor your efforts especially if you are launching several social media campaigns at once.

3. Post Frequently

It is very important to know how often and when you should post. If your target markets are those who are online during peak hours, then you should post during those times. If your target market includes those who go online during off peak hours then posting your campaigns within that duration is essential.

4. Post Quality Content

Another vital aspect that you must not overlook is the content of your posts. Text can be very boring and the fact that consumers these days prefer images means that incorporating images along with texts can serve your campaigns better. You may even use videos as people, in most cases, prefer to watch instead of read a full block of text.

CONTENT IS KING!

5. Make sure content echoes your brand's voice and values.

Whether you are posting a picture on Instagram or are tweeting an interesting article, all of the content that you post should clearly reflect your brand's voice and values. One of the easiest ways to do this is to establish a clear and concise mission statement, and guide all content creation around this mission statement.

And remember it's about what you can do for the follower, not what the follower can do for you. Starbucks is an excellent example of a brand doing this well. It is no secret that Starbucks is a social media giant, especially when it comes to Instagram and Facebook. The company's simple, consumer-driven mission statement—"To inspire and nurture the human spirit– one person, one cup and one neighborhood at a time–" is without a doubt one of the reasons why.

6. Create a content calendar.

One of the biggest social media blunders is sporadic posting. The key to enhancing social media visibility and facilitating consumer engagement is regular posting. If you abandon your social media accounts for weeks at a time your consumers are much less likely to find you relevant.

Once you have a timeline down for a campaign and have identified major milestones it is time to create a content calendar. Identify what you will be posting, which networks you want to publish to and when you will be posting it. Always include specific days and times.

Tools like MavSocial allow you to create a complete content calendar and then schedule your posts across multiple channels, to go at the times you selected.

7. Identify channel specific short-term and long-term objectives. The success of a social media campaign depends on its clarity and its precision. Identify what you are trying to achieve with each social media campaign. Are you trying to boost sales? Is the goal to increase visibility? Do you want more followers? Use short-term objectives as stepping-stones meet long-term goals so you can easily track progress.

CHAPTER FOUR

BENEFITS OF ADDING VISUAL CONTENTS TO YOUR SOCIAL MEDIA CAMPAIGNS

BENEFITS OF ADDING VISUAL CONTENTS TO YOUR SOCIAL MEDIA CAMPAIGNS

"Visual marketing does not just sell a product or service – it sells an experience around your business". –Rebekah Radice

When it comes to marketing content, the web is cluttered and competition is very high. Luckily, a great way to make your social media campaign stand out online is to make it more visual. Visual contents are not only easier and faster for the human brain to process, but are also a great way to attract more views, clicks and conversions.

Below are some interesting reasons why you should integrate visual content into your campaigns.

1. **Visual contents help to grab the attention of targeted audience.** This is why your content must be of a very high quality, very attractive and something that is easily memorable in order for you to be able to break through and capture the attention of your target audience.

2. Visual contents are usually processed faster by the human brain. The human brain can only process a very limited amount of information at any given time. Data that can be processed much faster takes precedence over those that cannot be processed fast when it comes to seizing people's attention.

3. Visual content makes up 93% of all human communication which is practically non-verbal. Likewise, 90% of information that enters the brain is practically non-verbal.

4. It generates more viewers for your contents and helps your platforms to gain new subscribers and followers.

5. Visual contents have the capacity to influence human emotions, they are more understandable and easy to relate with. Targeted audience can better understand your brand's message when you add detailed images and videos to your content.

6. Visual contents that go viral usually bring tons of inbound links to your website, especially if people like the content enough to like, share, retweet and comment on it.

7. Visual contents solicit targeted user action much more effectively, and get them to respond quickly than other plain and text-based contents.

SIX MISTAKES IN YOUR VISUAL CONTENT STRATEGY TO AVOID AND TOOLS TO FIX THEM

Your team may include a very good and talented graphic designer and highly skilled digital strategists, but crafting and sharing visual content on social media is an entirely different ball game entirely.

Do you know that when it's not done right, visual content has more than enough potential to be ignored? According to a 2013 Buffer study, Posts with images get 18% more clicks, 89% more likes and 150% more retweets on Twitter alone.

Below are mistakes you may likely make or have been making while crafting visual contents, and tools to help you correct them.

1. Posting Similar Images too frequently

Images with inspirational quotes may earn a click from a few followers, but your visual content strategy is limited if it is based on continuously sharing the same kinds of pictures.

To increase engagement, these visuals should be added to your content:

- **Screenshots:** Educational pictures of your product or service in action.

- **Infographics:** Visualizations of data or other helpful information typically long, but can be short and to-the-point for social media.
- **Preview Images:** Graphics that give a sneak peek at news, events or content.
- **Comic Strips:** Cartoons, whether funny or informative, that support your message.
- **Photographs:** Photos that add life to visual content strategies filled with graphics – can be stock or original.
- **Memes:** Popular image macros edited to bolster your post or reflect your brand – can certainly give your followers laughs.
- **GIFs:** Looping clips that are funny and relevant to earn likes and shares.
- **Video Clips:** Videos from YouTube, Periscope and other platforms embedded in your posts

The tool to use in achieving these is called **Canva.** This online image creation suite makes design easy with its intuitive interface. It gives you a library of layouts, illustrations, grids and photographs to play with.

2. Going Overboard with Color

A design with too much white space can look bare, but a busy color palette creates its own problems. That's because using too many bold tones makes images feel cluttered, and pairing oversaturated hues strains the eyes.

To avoid visual content that confuses your audience, stick to two or three colors and tints. Set on a neutral background tone, your choices should have enough contrast to pop and separate from each other.

The tool to use is called **Paletton.** Drag Paletton's color wheel cursor to create one-, three- or four-tone schemes.

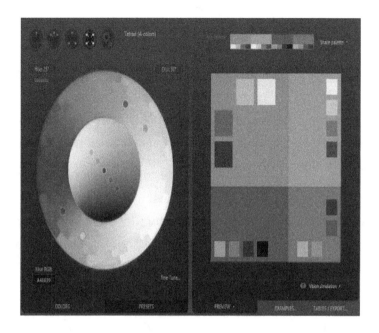

A palette will update on the right of your screen, giving you a look at how well your main color matches with the opposing or complementary ones. Just click on a box to see its RGB code, and design away in your image editor of choice.

3. Ignoring Your Website

Updating the visual content on your website should play a role in your social media strategy. That's because brands like yours aren't the largest sharers of images and videos; regular users are.

Almost 50% of adult Internet users share visual media they find when browsing websites, according to a 2013 Pew Research Center study. To boot, research from Curalate states 85% of the average brand's Pinterest presence comes from off-board user activity. By not including high-quality visuals – including headers, screenshots and tutorial images – you're missing a chance for third-party promotion.

The tool to use is WordPress. Almost a quarter of the websites you visit run on WordPress, according to the company's data. Along with thousands of themes to choose from, there's a collection of publishing and media management tools to post and optimize visual content. This makes it easier for visitors find and share your photos and videos.

4. Leaving Out Call to Actions

Leaving out a call-to-action (CTA) in your copy or image is a common mistake that hinders interaction. Followers often need encouragement to share or comment.

The best CTAs are short and specific. They should also start with verbs (click) or adverbs (quickly), according to research from Dan Zarrella:

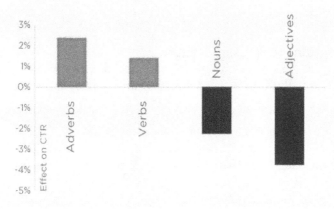

Use action words: more verbs, fewer nouns.

After analyzing 200,000 link containing tweets, I found that tweets that contained more adverbs and verbs had higher CTRs than noun and adjective heavy tweets.

5. Misrepresenting Your Brand

You don't have to use a logo to properly represent your brand. In fact, this can sometimes add clutter to your images. But without it, some social media accounts post content that lacks a clear connection to their products or services. Doing so can leave followers scratching their heads.

Visual content should reflect:

- What your brand stands for
- Your brand's unique or differentiating values
- The topics your audience is interested in.

After all, these three factors are probably the reason fans follow you.

6. Forgetting to Measure Results

Don't stay blind to what's working and what's not. Ignoring metrics is the first step in running a social media account that doesn't generate engagement or website traffic.

Based on data, tweak your visual content approach based on:

- Composition
- Posting Time
- CTA (Call-To-Action)
- Hashtag Use

After some testing, you'll discover the best design and posting strategies.

The tool to use is **Buffer.** Buffer is a popular social media scheduling tool, but it also tracks the numbers behind your posts. For example, it measures the likes, retweets, mentions and clicks each tweet earns. It also tracks potential – the number of people who could have viewed a tweet based on who shared it, the hashtags you use and your number of followers. Other tools that can help you measure your performance include Hootsuite, Feedly, SproutSocial, Google Analytics etc.

CHAPTER FIVE

TIPS FROM SOCIAL MEDIA MARKETING GENIUSES

TIPS FROM SOCIAL MEDIA MARKETING GENIUSES

"The goal of social media is to turn customers into a large volunteer army". –Jay Baer

Social media has incredibly become a very significant driving force in marketing. But the question is how the major companies do or brands make the most effective use of this very important tool?

In December 2014, in a report published by Shareaholic, top 8 social networks drove 31.24% of overall traffic to sites. No wonder more and more are people starting to understand the vital importance of social media in developing businesses online.

Your potential clients and customers are online across various social media platforms, so if you want to meet and engage them, you have to be where they are. Most importantly, keep in mind that if you still don't use social media to market your business, your competitors already do.

Here are a few stories of social marketing geniuses and experts across various platforms to inspire you.

1. Shane Martincik

In the social media world, the name Shane Martincik might not ring a bell. However, he is one of those few people using the power of social media to their and making cool cash in the process.

He started using social media when he was 15 years old. Firstly, to connect with friends, family and keeping up with trends. But unlike the people of his age, he had a greater yearning. He began to shift his mindset from a consumer to a producer.

In simple words, he developed an entrepreneurial mindset. Then, he started feeding his mind by surrounding himself with successful people with similar goals and interests so as to become what he is today.

Today, Shane is a master of social media marketing/advertising and currently in his fourth year of enjoying massive success as a teenager.

He didn't just become a success overnight. He started somewhere by taking one step at a time because he believed in himself and kept on pushing every day. He always showed up.

What Made Shane Martincik a Social Media Marketing Genius?

Shane's success can be attributed to pure hard work, determination and networking.

You know the saying that your network is your net worth? It's is true and Shane is a perfect example of this.

When he was starting the now successful educational company Pordo, he got introduced to a website designer who was working with a very successful social media person mogul then. Shane saw this as an opportunity to achieve one of his goals and then requested to be introduced so as to get acquainted and learn from him.

Because of his charisma, he was able to learn all what he needed to build large social media accounts on Instagram, Facebook, YouTube, Twitter etc. from his new friend within a short time.

He did all this by actively noting down everything he heard and saw him do. Then, he got to working on developing on those things he learnt and immediately started applying them. As he applied his new found skills, he knew that he was onto something massive.

As a young and seasoned entrepreneur, Shane started working on improving his skills so as to have an advantage over others and take over the social media space. He added what he had learnt to what he already knew and came up with his own unique system that worked.

He quickly figured out how to grow an Instagram account by 100 followers a day to 500 followers and even all the way to 5,000 followers a day. It was so unreal as how he could easily do this by improving the efficiency of his system just by reading between the lines.

As time went on, Shane went from being a teen without an Instagram account to a powerhouse with an account of over 100,000 Instagram followers all within 6 months! He was able to replicate his success with other social media like Pinterest, Twitter, Facebook, YouTube, Tumblr, Vine etc. The saying goes that if you use it, Shane probably abuses it!

Shane made his first million online by working hard and believing in his abilities. As a gift to his parents, he paid off their house mortgage.

For a 19 year old, Shane definitely knows what he's doing. And his secret to success in his own words is **LEVERAGE.** "If you can understand this, then you've the mindset of a millionaire and it'll be harder for you not to succeed".

If you can think it, you can achieve it. Always remember that your imagination equals possibilities.

2. Michael A. Stelzner

Michael Stelzner is a social media marketing leader, internet marketer, entrepreneur, author, and radio personality. He is the

CEO and Founder of Social Media Examiner, a media company that teaches people how to utilize social media platforms for their businesses.

He is also the creator of events hosted by Social Media Examiner, including the **Social Media Marketing World**.

In addition, he is the host of the **Social Media Marketing podcast**, the weekly **Morning Social Media Marketing Talk Show**, and an episodic video documentary called **The Journey**. He is also the founder of the **Social Media Marketing Society**.

He has written two books: *Writing White Papers* (2006) and *Launch* (2011).

Social Media Examiner

In the summer of 2009, Stelzner founded Social Media Examiner, a media company that teaches people how to utilize social media platforms for their businesses. They aim to help businesses learn how to best use social media to create relationships with customers, drive web traffic, generate outreach, and increase sales. His original idea was to start an online magazine or blog, writing detailed articles related to social media. His business partners, many of whom were writers and marketers, were not as excited about the experimental project.

After learning he was going to present at two major conventions in October that year, he hired web designers and illustrators to create a working website before then; they launched the website on October 12, 2009, two days before the convention. He attended one of the events with a video crew and interviewed a number of the social media gurus there, and uploaded the interviews over time throughout the month.

Within the first month, Social Media Examiner reached over 12,000 visitors. In less than five months, publisher advertising platform Technorati ranked them the #1 business blog in the world. As of February 2017, there are now 1.2 million people that read the blog.

3. Mark W. Schaefer

Mark Schaefer is a popular and quotable media resource for topics including:

- Social Media Trends

- Personal Branding

- Business Trends

- Twitter

- Social Media Marketing

- Influence Marketing

- Entrepreneurship

- Blogging

- Marketing Measurement

- Content Marketing

- Marketing Strategy

- Facebook

Mark is a globally-recognized speaker, educator, business consultant, and author who blogs at {grow} — one of the top marketing blogs of the world. He has worked in global sales, PR, and marketing positions for 30 years and now provides consulting services as Executive Director of U.S.-based Schaefer Marketing Solutions. He specializes in marketing strategy and social media workshops and clients include both start-ups and global brands such as Adidas, Cisco, Johnson & Johnson, Dell, Pfizer, The U.S. Air Force, and the UK government.

Mark has advanced degrees in marketing and organizational development and holds seven patents. He is a faculty member of the graduate studies program at Rutgers University and is the author of six best-selling marketing books: *KNOWN: The Handbook for Building and Unleashing your Personal Brand in the Digital Age; Social Media Explained; Return on Influence; Born to Blog; The Content Code; and The Tao of Twitter,* the *best-selling book on Twitter in the world. Return on Influence,* the first book on influence marketing, was named to the elite "Top Academic Titles" of the year by the American Library Association, which declared it an "essential" and "pathfinding" book. The *Content Code* was named one of the top five marketing books of 2015 by INC magazine. His books are used as textbooks at more than 50 universities, have been translated into 12 languages, and can be found in more than 750 libraries worldwide. He is the co-host of The Marketing Companion, one of the top 10 marketing podcasts on iTunes.

Mark is the seventh-most mentioned person by CMO's on Twitter and is among the Top 10 most re-tweeted marketing authorities in the world. He was listed as one of the Top 10 authorities on Social Selling by Forbes. His blog is in the top 1 percent of blogs in the world, based on number of reader comments. In 2015 he was named as the number two blogger in the world by Social Media Examiner and was named number one on a list compiled by Buffer. He is among the Top 10 Marketing Influencers in the world.

Mark is an entrepreneur and start-up advisor who recently launched a revolutionary new method to track and measure content marketing success. He has advanced degrees in both applied behavioral science and marketing, studying under Peter Drucker for three years.

He is among the world's most recognized social media marketing authorities and has been a keynote speaker at conferences such as Social Media Week London, SXSW, National Economic Development Association, Word of Mouth Marketing Conference Tokyo, National Association of State CIOs, and the Institute for International and European Affairs (an EU think tank). Mark has lectured at Oxford University, Carnegie-Mellon University, Princeton, and many other prestigious institutions.

Mark is a popular and entertaining commentator and has appeared on many national television shows and periodicals including the Wall Street Journal, Wired, The New York Times, CNN, National Public Radio, CNBC, the BBC and the CBS NEWS. He is a regular contributing columnist to The Harvard Business Review.

4. Amy Porterfield

She was just there to take notes.

A few years later, however, Amy Porterfield had built an online following of more than 250,000 entrepreneurs and created a 7 figure business for herself. Porterfield, best known for her top-ranked "Online Marketing Made Easy" Podcast and an array of online courses, recently shared on an episode of the Nemo Radio podcast how her whirlwind journey from working alongside Tony Robbins to striking out on her own as a first-time entrepreneur began.

A Fly on the Wall

Back in 2009, Porterfield was working as part of the content team for Bestselling Author, Speaker and Peak Performance Coach Tony Robbins.

"Tony had this meeting for the content team where he brought in some of the best online marketers around," Porterfield recalls. "And I was literally like a fly on the wall, sitting at a side table taking notes."

Bitten by the Entrepreneurial Bug

Inspired by what she was hearing - in particular about the lifestyle and freedom of choice enjoyed by these top online course creators and marketers - Porterfield's ears perked up.

"I knew nothing about the online marketing world at the time in terms of the level these guys were operating at," she recalls. "But I *knew* I had to be a part of it. So it was after that meeting when I caught the entrepreneurial bug."

Her newfound entrepreneurial fever was so strong that Porterfield decided to leave Robbins' company after more than six years to strike out on her own. After spending her first few years solo in the trenches executing online marketing and social media campaigns for clients, Porterfield eventually pivoted into creating online courses around topics like webinars, email list building and more.

Today, Porterfield presides over a business that does more than 7 figures annually in online course sales. She also revealed some of her biggest tips when it comes to building an engaged, ready-to-buy audience - whether you're a household name like Tony Robbins or a brand-new entrepreneur.

List Building 101: Know Thy Audience

"First, you have to start with knowing who your target audience is and creating a customer avatar," Porterfield says. "Because it's really hard to grow an email list if you don't know the *exact* type of person you want to attract."

Once you've figured out who it is you want to market to, according to Porterfield, one of the keys is to choose your core "lead magnet" wisely. For those unfamiliar with the term, a "lead magnet" is a free piece of content (an eBook, a free training video, etc.) that someone gets access to in exchange for sharing his or her email address. "You want to create a lead magnet that can cast a wide net," Porterfield says. "So it's not too specific in just one area for a certain portion of your target audience, but it's a topic that you think the majority of your avatar group would find valuable."

As an example, Porterfield utilizes a lead magnet for her Webinars That Convert online course that helps you determine the perfect (and most profitable) webinar topic. "Anybody who is interested in doing a webinar, one of the things that will stop him or her from getting started is being unsure of what topic to choose," Porterfield explains. "Or not having an idea for a great title.

"So I love the idea of having a core lead magnet that will meet you right where you're at, right now, helping you conquer a fear, challenge or obstacle that you face from the get go with this topic of webinars."

From there, Porterfield says, you can take a new email subscriber further into your content and sales funnel, sharing more tips and eventually selling your product or service to the person.

"But before you do that, you want your core lead magnet to address a question they have right now, *before* they're ever willing to buy from you," she adds.

The Golden Question

When she sets out to create a new lead magnet, Porterfield says she asks herself, "What does my core audience member need to know, understand or believe (related to this specific topic) before they're ever ready and willing to buy from me?"

When you think of it that way, Porterfield says, you can start with where your audience is at, instead of trying to force them into a place they're not ready to go with your initial lead magnet.

First and Most Important

Once you have a person on your email list, you must pay close attention to the very first email you deliver to the person, according to Porterfield.

Porterfield and her team call that first email you receive after signing up for one of her lead magnets the "what this says about you" message. "In that email, we deliver what we promise, meaning the lead magnet, but we also talk about where you're at, and let you know that we 'get' you, we understand you, we know the fears and struggles," she says. "We paint a picture of that helps you realize that we know where you're at right now, we've got you covered and we're going to take care of you."

Getting into the key beliefs, feelings and emotions that your core audience member is struggling with is critical to setting the right tone with your email exchanges, Porterfield says. "People have to feel as if you are a friend," she adds. "You want your audience to feel as if they have a friend in you."

Seeing is Believing

Porterfield has made plenty of friends since that day when she felt like a fly on the wall inside a meeting room with Tony Robbins and the world's top online marketers.

"It was so humbling, to just be in the room," she recalls. "I wasn't even at the main table. I was off to the side at a separate table, taking notes."

With a quarter of a million online entrepreneurs now hanging on her every word thanks to her list building strategies, it's safe to say Porterfield no longer has to worry about sitting on the sidelines when it comes to the online marketing space.

5. Eve Mayer Orsburn

Ranked by Forbes as the *Fifth Most Influential Woman in Social Media*, Eve Mayer is the CEO of Social Media Delivered, one of the most respected social media companies worldwide serving clients with consulting, training and outsourced social media. Eve has spoken in over 30 U.S. cities, as well as in Ireland, France, the UK and Iceland at universities, companies and conference groups, including Cisco, Vistage, Microsoft, Purdue, and Manchester Metropolitan University.

Eve is the author of *Social Media for the CEO* and *The Social Media Business Equation*. Her groundbreaking work in social media has been featured on American Express Open Forum, CIO.com, Forbes, Social Media Today, Mashable, Huffington Post and many others. Recognized by Webbiquity as one of the *Top 50 Women on Twitter,* and by CNN as one of the *8 Women on Twitter Who Will Inspire, Inform and Amuse You,* she shares her social media knowledge with a network of over 100,000 fans and followers. She has also been ranked number 7 on the most powerful women social media influencers and ranked 14th on the overall social media power influencer list according to Forbes.

Eve is known as @LinkedinQueen because of her knowledge of leveraging LinkedIn for B2B sales and recruiting, and Klout even ranks her as the 2nd Most Influential Person on the subject of LinkedIn, behind only LinkedIn itself. Eve has been nominated for numerous Women Owned Business Awards in the past few years in recognition of her achievements.

6. Deirdre Breakenridge

Deirdre Breakenridge (born 1966 in Englewood, New Jersey) is an American University professor, author, public speaker, entrepreneur and CEO of Pure Performance Communications.

Breakenridge is teaching on the graduate and undergraduate level at New York University (NYU), University of Massachusetts Amherst, Rutgers University and Fairleigh Dickinson University (FDU).

Breakenridge speaks nationally and internationally on the topics of PR, marketing, branding and social media.

Breakenridge is the co-founder of #PRStudChat, a dynamic twitter chat with PR professionals, educators and students. She hosts the podcast show, Women Worldwide, produced by the Social Network Station. She was awarded the Best 50 Women in Business by NJBIZ in 2015, named on the Richtopia 250 Most Influential Women Leaders in the World List, recognized by Cision as one of the Top 50 Social Media influencers in 2014, and 2014 PR Tech Award honoree.

Deirdre has appeared on NBC, WMCN as well as other media outlets. In addition, she has been featured in FOXNews.com, Fast Company, Entrepreneur, Inc., CIO, Huffington Post, Wall Street Journal and Mashable.

As an adjunct professor at NYU, she teaches a social media objectives and strategies class for the Graduate Public Relations & Corporate Communications Program. She also teaches a social media certificate course at Pratt Institute in New York. Breakenridge speaks nationally and internationally on the topics of PR, marketing and social media communications. In 2012, she was a keynote speaker at the Social Conference in Amsterdam, delivered the keynote address for the Canadian Public Relations Society (CPRS) Annual Conference, and presented the keynote at the PRSA Southwest District Conference in Tulsa, Oklahoma. Breakenridge has also presented at the International Public Relations Association (IPRA), BlogWorld and The Public Relations Institute of Australia (PRIA).

7. Mari Smith

In February of 1999, Mari Smith needed a sign from the universe. It showed up in the form of ... cake.

The Scottish-Canadian had arrived in San Diego on a borrowed round-trip plane ticket ("That's how broke I was!") with 50 British pounds in her pocket and a feeling that she was supposed to start her nascent seminar business in the U.S. instead of Scotland, her former home.

But she was running out of time. She could only come into the country for 30 days without all her immigration paperwork done, and her deadline was looming.

"I absolutely knew I wasn't going to go back," she recalls. "I remember saying to the universe: 'It's been 4 weeks. I know I'm supposed to stay here. Just give me a sign.'"

Two hours later, a local bakery whose door Mari had knocked on (her father was a baker, from whom she had picked up a few tips as well as attending confectionery classes for a few years) called to see if she could come in and decorate cakes before the Valentine's Day rush.

Known as the Queen of Facebook, she says, "Facebook kind of landed in my lap at a time that was perfect for how I was evolving my business and my talents. It was really a beautiful unfolding, a beautiful merging of two primary themes throughout my whole career: my love of people, my love of technology.

"In the early 2000s I was working successfully as a business consultant. In 2007 I got an invitation to be on a beta test team of an app called Podclass, a site where you can take and teach classes. To be honest, I was a little reluctant at first. When Facebook came along, I was like, not another social network! But when I opened up the site, I have to tell you it was one of those defining moments in life.

"I could feel the vibe jumping off the screen. I thought, wait a second. This is nothing like MySpace, it doesn't feel like LinkedIn. This feels unique and different.

"What excited me more than anything is that people who I'd long admired for years, read their books, famous people, people I really looked up to, all of a sudden I'm befriending them on Facebook and we're chitchatting and I was able to interview them.

"Today, Facebook now encompasses such a comprehensive range of skills that marketers need to have that it's caught people by surprise. It's not just about creating good content or driving them to your site. Now it's got to be good sales copy, you've got to be good at crafting ads, you've got to get people to click, and you also have to have a super compelling landing page, a compelling offer, and you've got to be reaching the right market. There are a lot of components that people have to wrap their arms around".

8. Brian Carter

Brian Carter (born July 15, 1973) is an American author, speaker, marketer and comedian. He also is the CEO of The Carter Group, a digital marketing and advertising agency.

Brian is a digital marketing expert and has developed marking programs for Microsoft, Universal Studios, the United States Army and Hardee's. He was included on Everything PR's list of "Top 50 PR Professionals You Should Be Following On Twitter" in July 2011. That year, Carter was quoted in *Twitter Marketing For Dummies*, a book discussing what Twitter is and how to use it for marketing. He has also been featured in *The Wall Street Journal*, a segment on ABC News, Bloomberg Television, *Forbes*, Mashable, and the U.S. News & World Report.

Carter has written for marketing blogs including Social Media Examiner, Mashable, Convince & Convert, Search Engine Journal and AllFacebook. He has spoken at Social Media Marketing World, Moz, SMX, Pubcon, The AllFacebook Expo and Socialize and The American Marketing Association. In 2014, Stryde included Carter on its list of "Top 50 Social Media Experts."

9. Dan Zarrella

Dan Zarrella is the award-winning social media scientist and author of four books: *The Science of Marketing*, *Zarrella's Hierarchy of Contagiousness*, *The Social Media Marketing Book*, and *The Facebook Marketing Book.*

He has a background in web development and combines his programming capabilities with a passion for social marketing to study social media behavior from a data-backed position and teach marketers scientifically grounded best practices. One of the first marketers at HubSpot, he spent 6 years at the company, watching it grow from startup to big, public company.

Webinars in his "Science of..." series have drawn upwards of 30,000 registrants. And he holds the Guinness World Record for the largest webinar ever. His Science of ReTweets Report analyzes the when, why and how Twitter users ReTweet things, and explains how marketers can effectively get more ReTweets, and TweetPsych is linguistic analysis tool he built that allows users to generate psychological profiles of any other Twitter user or list based on the contents of their Tweets.

He served as a member of the Boston's City Council's Citizens' Committee on Boston's Future and has been featured in The New York Times, The Wall Street Journal, The Boston Globe, Wired, Fast Company, Forbes, The Financial Times, Huffington Post, The London Times, The Miami Herald, Slashdot, Smart Money, AdAge, NYPost, The Atlantic, Mashable, The Twitter

Book, and TechCrunch. In 2009 he was awarded Shorty and Semmy awards for social media & viral marketing.

He has spoken at numerous conferences, including: PubCon, SXSW, SES, SMX, Iowatasmic, Convergence '09, 140 The Twitter Conference, The Cool Twitter Conference, WordCamp Mid Atlantic, Social Media Camp, Inbound Marketing Bootcamp, and Social Fresh.

10. Pam Moore

Pam Moore is one of the most in-demand international keynote speakers in the world. Pam has presented for IBM, Lowe's Home Improvement, GolfWeek, British Council, Sony Playstation, Polish Insurance Association, Chick-Fil-A, Caribbean Association of Corporate Counsel, International Classified Media Association, Social Media Marketing World, Hubspot Inbound, Social Media Strategies Summit and numerous other brands and conferences.

Pam is ranked by Forbes as a Top 10 Social Media Power Influencer, Top 10 Digital Marketers to Follow on Twitter, Top 10 most retweeted by digital marketers and the list goes on.

She is the CEO and co-founder of Marketing Nutz, a full service social media, branding and digital marketing training and consulting agency that specializes in helping businesses of all sizes select, leverage and optimize social and digital technologies to achieve their business goals. She is a bestselling author with 20 years of experiences helping entrepreneurs to Fortune 100 organizations build winning brands, and integrated platforms that deliver measurable results.

Before becoming an entrepreneur and founding her first digital marketing agency (that sold in less than 2 years), Pam spent 15+ years working in corporate marketing and product management for organizations such as Hitachi Data Systems, GE Capital, Sun Microsystems, Storagetek, and IBM as a digital marketing and change agent helping organizations integrate new technologies and media to better excel in the digital online world. Her methodologies have been adopted by brands around the globe.

Pam has a zest for life, and helping bridge the digital divide to help human beings connect with one another in authentic ways. Pam leaves her audiences feeling energized and empowered to take on the always changing world of technology.

When she presents as a keynote speaker for your event she brings her virtual audience with her to help you increase event sales, ignite your audience and build a lasting community.

With more than 285,000 engaged Twitter followers, top of iTunes charts Podcast – Social Zoom Factor generating more than 100,000 downloads per month, active blogging community, weekly Tweet chats (#GetRealChat) delivering 40-90+ million impressions weekly, Pam is globally recognized as one of the most prominent thought leaders on the subject of social and new media as it relates to business.

Her work has been noted in Forbes, Huffington Post, Entrepreneur, Yahoo! News, Business Insider, Inc., USA Today, Inc, Orlando Sentinal, Orlando Business Journal, Social Media Today, Business to Community and many more.

Here are **20 tips** experts in social media marketing have come up with that can help you maximize the effectiveness of social media campaigns:

1. **Regular posting** – The more posts you put out there for your audience to see and follow, the more trust you will be able to build over time.

2. **Deliver relevant content** – Always make sure that what your audience hears and sees is interesting and agrees with your brand identity.

3. **Always make your content unique** – Try to avoid repetition of contents. If you want to stand out on social media platforms, make sure your content is unique to your brand.

4. **Share and retweet other people's content** - This can be a great way to demonstrate to your audience that you know what is relevant.

5. **Be as visible as possible** – Don't be afraid to follow some of your competitors and even interact with their content.

6. **Offer help** – Endeavour to respond on Twitter, Facebook or any other platform whenever you have legitimate answers to questions, and never follow up with calls to action or sales language. Be genuine about wanting to help.

7. **Learn from your mistakes** – Using analytics tools, analyze your past posts to determine what works consistently and what

doesn't. Refrain from posting contents that fail to get significant engagement.

8. Always use visual contents on social media – Use images and videos to your maximum advantage as they get better engagements than plain texts.

9. Stop fishing for likes and shares – Try engaging your audience in ways that encourage conversations and interactions. If people find what you post interesting, they will naturally share it.

10. Host live hangouts – This makes the social media experience look more real. Both Google hangouts and live Twitter events are great tools to use.

11. Make strategic use of hashtags on all social media platforms where they are helpful – Don't just come up with hashtags to add to your posts whenever you want to include them in your content. You should thoroughly research trending hashtags. There are times when you can trend but if you want to broaden your reach, you need to follow existing trends.

12. Automate whatever you can – To ensure a fresh flow of content, use automation tools to schedule your posts and keep your content organized.

13. Keep track of what your competitors are posting – Look out for patterns in your competitors' content, and test out similar materials on your own.

14. **Hold contests and giveaways** – Very few things churn up the kind of buzz that is created by giving away freebies, so always consider some friendly competition among your followers.

15. **Use your email list to promote your social media content** – This can be a great way to drive targeted traffic to your social media platforms.

16. **Encourage employee engagement on your channels** – The people that are working in your organization are your best endorsers. Enlist their help in sharing your content on their individual platforms.

17. **Become an authority** – Position yourself as a leader in your niche and post contents that prove you as a leader.

18. **Take risks** – Try something strange or new once in a while and never be afraid to stretch people's perception of your brand.

19. **Know your audience** – Listen to them, be useful to them, serve them and invest in them. This usually pays in the long run.

20. **When writing content for your company**, always ask yourself how your content helps your customers.

CHAPTER SIX

CHARACTERISTICS OF A SUCCESSFUL SOCIAL MEDIA CAMPAIGN

CHARACTERISTICS OF A SUCCESSFUL SOCIAL MEDIA CAMPAIGN

"Good marketing makes the company look good. Great marketing makes the customer feel smart". –
Joe Chernov

S ocial media can be a great way to increase brand awareness, customer engagement and long-term loyalty, and generate a long-term boost in sales, but it's also a potential minefield and in the worst case, a bottomless pit into which you endlessly shovel money with nothing much to show for it. All successful social media campaigns have a few things in common, which every small business owner should be aware of as he or she considers how to maximize their potential on the Internet. With the continuing growth of social media in the marketing world, there is no denying that this medium can be an influential tool for branding a business and interacting with consumers.

To make certain your social media campaign becomes a great success, here are eight characteristics of effective social media campaigns.

1. KNOW YOUR TARGET

Social media campaigns come in different forms and every campaign is distinctive. But what all successful social media campaigns have in common is a clear set of goals and objectives. You need to take time to think through what you are trying to achieve and the target audience you want to engage. Without this, your chances of success are going to be slim to zero.

- Is your main goal to increase brand awareness by reaching out to a new target audience or is it more about educating, informing and engaging existing customers?
- Is your goal to generate information about a new product launch or event?
- Is your goal to increase sales of an underperforming product line?

2. MAKE USE OF CAPTIVATING VISUALS

Social media campaigns cannot be successful without the use of captivating and attractive visuals. You're going to need first-rate visuals to really grab the attention of your target audience. Posting texts and links to articles won't be enough to create a buzz about your brand in the social media market. Not every social media campaign is about generating direct sales and there are plenty of ways to run other types of successful social media campaigns using visuals. It's not that text isn't important; it's more about giving a face to your company. Your target audience needs to know that your company is run by real people. You can do that by uploading photos of your team or pictures and videos of your company events.

3. DON'T UNDERESTIMATE THE POWER OF GREAT CONTENT

If you want your campaign to stand out, having good content is one of the strategies to use to get the attention of your users. The cornerstone of any effective social media campaign is great content presented in an interesting and engaging way. Make yourself the place where customers come for advice. To help yourself do better, put yourself in the customer's shoes, ask and address questions that you would like answered. It leads to more traffic and is considered as one of the best ways by experts.

4. USE SOCIAL MEDIA PLATFORMS TO INTERACT WITH YOUR TARGET AUDIENCE.

Regular posting on social media platforms is just not adequate; you need to engage your audience as well. This means answering their questions, posting encouraging comments, and rousing excitement among your followers. Social media platforms can be optimally used to address customer's service issues. Make sure you make it easier for users to find you using appropriate tags, etc.

There are several social media networks. You need to use all the available ones to your advantage. Confining yourself to only one platform like Facebook for example, is not a very good idea. You can target and reach out to a wider audience if you use other networking sites such as Twitter, Instagram and Pinterest.

5. POST FREQUENTLY AT OPTIMAL TIMES

It is very important for you to post regularly. Not once a week or once a month, but on a more consistent basis, for example, every day at a specific time. Use an appropriate fan page name or Twitter handle. Make sure that your fan page on Facebook or handle on Twitter is as close to the name of your company as possible. This will prevent any confusion and also make it easier for your audience to search for you. For your campaign to be successful you have to ensure your target audience knows about it.

Posting once a week or even twice a week is not enough. Knowing the best time can help you optimize when you post to your social networks. You have to be strategic about when you post and how often you do it. It's up to you to figure out the right time to post – and also how frequently to do so. Social media tools like Buffer or Hoot Suite can help you schedule your posts in advance if you're afraid you won't have time to do it each day.

6. USE THE RIGHT MEDIUM FOR YOUR MESSAGE

A great message helps your campaigns stand out from the rest. However, having a great message isn't enough; you also have to communicate it through the right channels. Using the right medium should not be limited to Facebook, and YouTube. You can target and reach out to a wider audience if you use other networking sites such as Twitter, Instagram and Pinterest. There are also various media but if that's not where your target audience hangs out it isn't going to do you much good. It also pays to remember that people tend to act in different ways on different networks so think about the manner you want your users to take and match the medium to the message.

7. ANALYTIC TOOLS ARE VITAL

You should always monitor how your campaigns are doing. With the help of analytical tools, you'll get to keep track of your posts, images or videos and see how they are performing. You can even check which ones are being shared to others the most. Several third-party programs will help you do this and using some of the best ones will help you monitor your efforts especially if you are launching several social media campaigns at once.

8. INTEGRATE EMAIL MARKETING

Email marketing is directly marketing a commercial message to a group of people using email. In its broadest sense, every email sent to a potential or current customer could be considered email marketing. It usually involves using email to send ads, request business, or solicit sales or donations, and is meant to build loyalty, trust, or brand awareness. Email marketing can be done to either sold lists or a current customer database. It is one of the best channels for a successful social media campaign. It is still one of the most effective places to reach a customer, and you can easily turn a social media graphic into an email graphic. You can either create separate promo codes so that you know how many people responded to your campaign by channel or you can use the same promo code for the entire campaign across both channels.

CHAPTER SEVEN

STRATEGIES FOR ENGAGING THE SOCIAL MEDIA AS A MARKETING TOOL

STRATEGIES FOR ENGAGING THE SOCIAL MEDIA AS A MARKETING TOOL

"Without a clear strategy in place, tools won't make any difference to you". –Ian Cleary

Social media is one of the most powerful tools in marketing your products. If you use it well, you can create a strong personal connection with your prospective clients. However, marketers often make the mistake of using social media without a clear plan. At best, this is a waste of time. To benefit from social media, you need to build a clear strategy that takes into account what you're trying to achieve, who your customers are and what your competition is doing. Have you ever wondered how people became "The Experts" in social media marketing? If you want to know their secrets, then you will find the information presented below extremely useful.

1. Have clear business goals and objectives

Every business venture needs to have a goal. You have to ask yourself why you want to use social media as your marketing tool. What do you want to achieve? Do you wish to have better recognition? Do you want to improve your branding? Don't start if you still haven't found the answers to these questions.

2. Increase online presence on more Social Media networks

Increasing your presence on various social media platforms is one great strategy of social media marketing, Aside from Facebook and Twitter (another dominant social media force), there are new and upcoming social media networks that are gradually gaining ground in the social market Among these upcoming social networks, Google+ and Instagram have gained tremendous ground and have overtaken other networks.

Other social networks are also gaining ground, many of which are focusing on graphics, pictures and videos as main focus for content. This includes Pinterest, Vine and Snapchat among others, each focusing on certain user categories and demographics. If you want maximum exposure for your business, it would be wise to develop a strong social media presence not only on Facebook and Twitter but on other social media networks as well.

3. Modify Your Content According to Specific Social Media Platform

If you want to attract customers and increase your sales, you need to provide great and high quality content to your audience, the type of content that will inform them of just how useful and relevant your products or services are to them. Highlight its benefits instead of its features when presenting your campaigns or deals and explain why your followers need to buy it.

Don't make the error of posting the same content through all the social networks they belong to. By doing so, business fail in delivering the unique user experience social media users are looking for from each particular platform. People who use Pinterest and Instagram often are more interested in content with visual and will be more attracted to really high-quality pictures and graphics that tell your story. The key to success in this regard is to ensure that your content suits each particular social media platform – and check which format will work best.

4. Organize contests and promotional activities

One of the most effective strategies for social media in general is to get your targeted audience directly involved in activities. Conducting contests and other promotional activities are perfect ways of driving their interests and soliciting their participation. You can be as creative as you can be in the type of contests you conduct, but making use of the sharing and other viral components available in your social network can bring even more exposure for your brand or business as more and more online users join in.

5. Share more pictures and graphics, and video content

Never underestimate the power of graphics and video content. That's the power of video and other visual elements and learning how to harness the power of these tools and elements can give you maximum exposure for your business. Now, micro-video is slowly gaining ground, providing yet another form of content that will change the social media sphere. Snapchat, Twitter's Vine, and the new micro-video sharing feature in Instagram will definitely gain more usage, now that such video sharing activities can be done through smartphones and other Internet-enabled mobile devices.

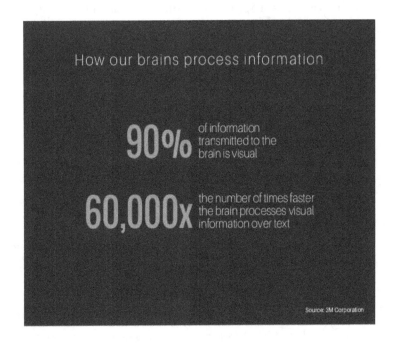

How our brains process information

90% of information transmitted to the brain is visual

60,000x the number of times faster the brain processes visual information over text

Source: 3M Corporation

6. Give out a lot of free trials and deals/discounts

A free trial or deal brings the clients in and keeps them there. Giving discounts off your regular charges will prove valuable for your targeted clients and the chances of them becoming loyal customers while your business exists can go much higher if you give lots of freebies on a regular basis.

Free deals don't mean giving your main products away. Freebies may be useful articles, free webinars, free videos, and a host of other content that you can give away for free. The more your targeted audiences receive these freebies, the more they can get to know the value of your brand until such time that they transition into paying customers.

7. Be more detailed

Attract your targeted audience. People love stories and they go to social media networks to read stories, be amazed with interesting features, and learn new things from uploads and shares. To use social media effectively, you must learn how to tell a story first before you can even sell stuff.

When you tell stories, people will get interested in you and your brand. They would want to know more about you and thus want to read, view or watch more stories, pictures and videos about you. There will come a time when their level of interest has grown to the right proportions that they can now be interested in your business, in what you do and in what you sell – and this will be the right time for profits to come rolling in.

8. Reply all comments, suggestions, and complaints.

Social media users comment, suggest, inquire or even complain on business pages and social media profiles. They do this and expect you or your social media manager to give them some form of response or acknowledgement. Social media is "social" and users expect some form of interaction from business owners and digital marketers.

Those who respond to these comments and inquiries will automatically be in a competitive advantage over other businesses or digital marketers who do not. You should also know how to handle or address complaints with proper responses that will satisfy online users. Do not delete these complaints or these users will delete you from their lists. On top of that, always show your gratitude for the time spent by online users in reading, liking, or sharing your posts and content. Doing so will put you in their favor and there will be more than likely chances that they will come back, read more of your content, and even let others know about you and your brand as well.

GO WIN ON ALL SIDES BY PRACTISING ALL THESE!

Stephen Akintayo, an inspirational speaker and Serial Entrepreneur is currently the Chief Executive Officer of Stephen Akintayo Consulting International and Gtext Media and Investment Limited, a leading firm in Nigeria whose services span from Digital Marketing, Website Design, Bulk SMS, Online Advertising, Media, E-Commerce, Real Estate,Consulting and a host of other services.

Stephen, Also Founded GileadBalm Group Services which has assisted a number of businesses in Nigeria to move to enviable levels by helping them reach their clients through its enormous nationwide data base of real phone numbers and email addresses. It has hundreds of organizations as its clients including multinational companies like Guarantee Trust Bank, PZ Cussons, MTN, Chivita, among others.
Stephen, popularly called Pastor Stephen is also the founder of Omonaija, an online radio station and SAtv in Lagos currently streaming for 24 hours daily with the capacity to reach every country of the world.

To invite **Stephen Akintayo** for a speaking engagement kindly visit

stephenakintayo.com/bookings
email: invite@stephenakintayo.com or
call: 0818 811 1999